LIFE JOURNALING

A Process of Finding Inner Harmony

Dr. Norman R. Wise
Executive Director of
Living Water Life Coaching

livingwatercoaching.com

Redeemer Publishing

Contents

Introduction

This journal is designed to help us learn a process of thinking about problems, proposals and propositions that we face and find ways to, process, analyze, develop and harmonize our thoughts so that we can find practical solutions to issues we face in our lives and find peace concerning them.

I began journaling over thirty years ago. I have kept all types of journals and they have had a significant impact on keeping me sane, stable and spiritual. This particular journal guides us in the application of a type of journaling that may help us sort out our thoughts, make wise decisions, process our emotions and have less stress.

This process was inspired by Dr. Lou Marinoff and his book **Plato Not Prozac**! In it he developed what he called philosophical counseling. I was very impressed by his method and while experimenting with it found something very practical that could be helpful to many if broken down into a very concrete practice. I have made my own alterations and changes to Dr. Marinoffs original concepts but I am indebted to him for my inspiration and general approach. I would highly recommend the reading of his book since it has a very interesting outlook.

What is the P.E.A.C.E. process?

Part of what causes stress in our life is disorganized, chaotic, confused, and random thinking. The P.E.A.C.E. process used in this journal can be very helpful in moving from this stressful mind frame to one that is organized, structured, rational, stable and systematic.

What is the P.E.A.C.E. process? It is a systematic way of slowing our thinking down and allowing us to harmonize and organize our thoughts. It lays the foundation for good decision-making and for the acceptance of events outside of our control. P.E.A.C.E. stands for the following five-step process:

Problem
Emotion
Analyze
Contemplate
Experiment

Notes

The process begins with defining the problem, perplexity, or troubling proposition we are struggling with. It also means choosing one of these to think about at a time. We can only really think well when we are thinking about one thing. Therefore, we need to slow down our thinking and think about one important issue in our life at a time. This part of the process asks us to focus our attention on one issue only and to define exactly what it is.

The next step in the process is to express and explore the emotions that this problem, perplexity, or proposition is stirring up in us. We need to allow ourselves to name and claim the emotions that are in our inner world. This allows us to begin to determine if our emotions seem appropriate or exaggerated over the issue we are facing. How are our emotions keeping us from working through our problems or how are they helping us resolve our issues? How could this problem have triggered unresolved issues from our past?

Once we have defined our emotions we then what to analyze our options. We need to logically and rationally list every possible solution to our problem without prejudice. At this point it does not matter if we believe or do not believe any of these potential answers will work, it is only necessary that we list them. We need to be totally honest and even put down the possible answers that we do not like.

This is like "internal brainstorming" where we imagine there is a group of people at a table and everyone is being asked to present every idea they have on how to handle the problem, perplexity, or proposition we have defined. In this imaginary situation we need to see that our job is to listen to everyone around the table and just write down every idea we hear without judgment or comment.

Once we have done this we need to choose between three and six solutions that seem to us to be the best possible answers. If we want we can make one of these purposely be one that we don't like, just to make sure we are being honest. Then list under each of these the strengths and weaknesses of each answer. We again need to do this as objectively and fairly as we can without prejudice to which answer we "like".

The next step is to now to contemplate our analysis. Looking at our answers, which seems logically and rationally to provide us with the best solution to our struggle? We now need to commit ourselves to this one answer or even develop a new hybrid from those we originally thought about. The key here is to decide on what we believe to be the best answer we can to the problem we now face. What would be the impact actually applying this answer to our current lifestyle?

The last step is to develop an experiment to test our answer. We may want to go back and make sure our answer really fits our original problem and that it relates to our emotions. Once we are satisfied we have stayed on target then we need to think about what small but real change we could make that would take our thinking into the world of action. How could we change our habitual way of handling this problem with the solution we have developed? This allows our inner thinking and our outer world to be in harmony and this creates peace.

By using this process to guide our journaling then we will find that we can have greater inner peace as we process the problems, perplexities, and difficult propositions which we all face in our lives. It will slow our inner thoughts down and help them have structure and harmony. This will lower our stress and increase our sense of inner peace.

Now I would also recommend we always approach this process in a prayerful attitude. For prayer is a vital part of finding inner peace. As the Apostle Paul wrote:

> ESV **Philippians 4:5** Let your reasonableness be known to everyone. The Lord is at hand; 6 do not be anxious about anything, but in everything by prayer and supplication with thanksgiving let your requests be made known to God. 7 And the peace of God, which surpasses all understanding, will guard your hearts and your minds in Christ Jesus. 8 Finally, brothers, whatever is true, whatever is honorable, whatever is just, whatever is pure, whatever is lovely, whatever is commendable, if there is any excellence, if there is anything worthy of praise, think about these things.

The P.E.A.C.E. process is an attempt for us to be reasonable and to know the peace of logical and honest thinking about issues in our lives. Everyone will know people who use the P.E.A.C.E. process on a regular basis as reasonable people. After this it is vital for us to release to God the anxiety we will still have over the problems we face and even over the outcome of the experiment we have committed ourselves to trying to make the situation better. This type of prayer of release is a vital part of what should also be done in the process since it will help us to be not just sane but also stable and spiritual.

After we have released our fears to God in prayer it is important we direct and focus our thoughts upon the positive realities of our life and the great wonderful potentials of our future as God leads us on a daily basis. Paul makes clear that we should not allow negative thoughts to dominate our thinking but rather put our emphasis on the positive truths of His love, His plan, and His oversight of our lives due to His love for us in Christ Jesus our Lord.

Now some of us may not believe very much in prayer. Or have doubts about the positive realities of life. This is an area that we would need to explore, study, expand, and experiment with in order to allow it to be part of our process. For me it is a vital part of the over all process.

With this general outline of the process the best place way to start is by actually beginning the P.E.A.C.E. process and the practice of journaling. It is by doing this that you will learn it. So let us begin the process.

Problem
Emotion
Analyze
Contemplate
Experiment

Prayer for Inner Peace

God grant me the serenity
to accept the things I cannot change;
courage to change the things I can;
and wisdom to know the difference.

Living one day at a time;
Enjoying one moment at a time;
Accepting hardships as the pathway to peace;
Taking, as He did, this sinful world
as it is, not as I would have it;
Trusting that He will make all things right
if I surrender to His Will;
That I may be reasonably happy in this life
and supremely happy with Him
Forever in the next.
Amen.

— Reinhold Niebuhr

P - Step one: Defining the Problem, perplexity, or troubling proposition.

Our first step is to define which problem, perplexity, or troubling proposition we would like to work on. This can sometimes be hard because we feel so overwhelmed with many complex and interrelated issues it is hard to single out one problem or struggle we may be facing.

First we face real problems. These problems can be very objective or subjective. However they are very real to us. In some cases we may have bewilderment, confusion, or perplexity. Or we may have some troubling idea or belief that is driving from us inner harmony and peace. Here we allow ourselves to define, dissect, and determine what these issues are and write them down. The very act of writing them down will make them seem smaller and more manageable then they feel when they are in our minds.

We can if we want start with a “Master Problem List” in which we simply write down every single problem, perplexity, and troubling proposition that we have. This is a type of “problem vomit” in which we are committing to paper all those things that are troubling us. Once we have done this we can choose one of these problems to process. Or if we don’t want or feel we can make a master problem list, we can just start off with one particular problem that we are focused on at the present moment.

MASTER PROBLEM LIST:

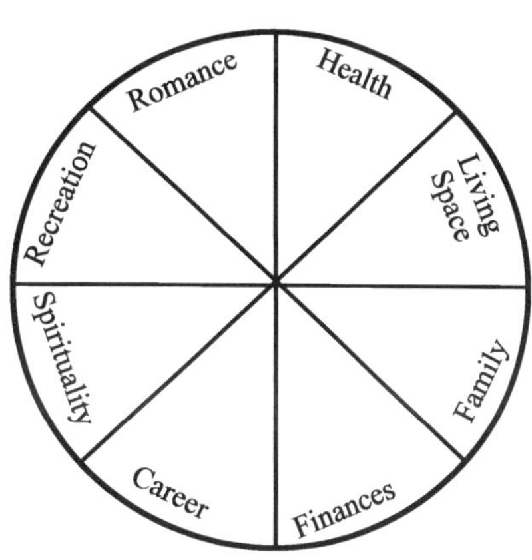

On this page

Draw a large circle

Divide the circle into 8 segments or so – like a pizza – where each piece represents an area of your life as it is now.

Label each piece with the parts of your life. These may include.

- **Spiritual and Study** - Church, prayer, Bible study, spiritual disciplines, service, encounter with God, reading great books.
- **Emotions** – How am I feeling? Happiness, depression, focused, confused, stable, chaotic
- **Calling in a Career** - Job satisfaction, career path, degrees to gain a position we feel called to achieve.
- **Relationships & Family** – Spouse, fiancée, children, parents, relatives
- **Social** - Friends, sports, activities
- **Health** - Exercise, diet
- **Financial** - Savings, investments
- **Fun & Creative** - Self-space, Sports, artistic , hobbies

Draw Circle here:

Beginning with each slice of your pie, list the problems, perplexities, or beliefs that you have in that area. Or just randomly write them down and then go back and put a number or label by each one indicating which part of your life this problem would belong. Separate each problem with a blank line.

List your problems here:

PROBLEM DEFINITION WORKSHEETS

How do I define my problem?

What caused you to think there was a problem?

What is perplexing, baffling; confusing; complicated about this issue?

What makes this issue a problem?

How would I describe this problem or issue to my best friend?

How critical is it to you that you find an answer to this problem?

What about this problem takes away your peace?

Is there a problem underneath this problem that is the real problem? What is that problem?

What would be the opposite of having this problem?

"A clever person solves a problem.
A wise person avoids it."
Albert Einstein

Define Your Problem

How do I define my problem?

What caused you to think there was a problem?

What is perplexing, baffling; confusing; complicated about this issue?

What makes this issue a problem?

How would I describe this problem or issue to my best friend?

How critical is it to you that you find an answer to this problem?

What about this problem takes away your peace?

Is there a problem underneath this problem that is the real problem? What is that problem?

What would be the opposite of having this problem?

"If you only have a hammer, you tend to see every problem as a nail."
Abraham Maslow

Define Your Problem

How do I define my problem?

What caused you to think there was a problem?

What is perplexing, baffling; confusing; complicated about this issue?

What makes this issue a problem?

How would I describe this problem or issue to my best friend?

How critical is it to you that you find an answer to this problem?

What about this problem takes away your peace?

Is there a problem underneath this problem that is the real problem? What is that problem?

What would be the opposite of having this problem?

"Never let a problem become an excuse."
Robert Schuller

Define Your Problem

How do I define my problem?

What caused you to think there was a problem?

What is perplexing, baffling; confusing; complicated about this issue?

What makes this issue a problem?

How would I describe this problem or issue to my best friend?

How critical is it to you that you find an answer to this problem?

What about this problem takes away your peace?

Is there a problem underneath this problem that is the real problem? What is that problem?

What would be the opposite of having this problem?

"As the problems are new,
we must disenthrall ourselves from the past."
Abraham Lincoln

Define Your Problem

How do I define my problem?

What caused you to think there was a problem?

What is perplexing, baffling; confusing; complicated about this issue?

What makes this issue a problem?

How would I describe this problem or issue to my best friend?

How critical is it to you that you find an answer to this problem?

What about this problem takes away your peace?

Is there a problem underneath this problem that is the real problem? What is that problem?

What would be the opposite of having this problem?

"It isn't that they can't see the solution. It is that they can't see the problem."

G K Chesterton

Define Your Problem

How do I define my problem?

What caused you to think there was a problem?

What is perplexing, baffling; confusing; complicated about this issue?

What makes this issue a problem?

How would I describe this problem or issue to my best friend?

How critical is it to you that you find an answer to this problem?

What about this problem takes away your peace?

Is there a problem underneath this problem that is the real problem? What is that problem?

What would be the opposite of having this problem?

"It's much easier to suggest solutions when you don't know too much about the problem."
Malcolm Forbes

Define Your Problem

**"The problems of victory are more agreeable than those of defeat,
but they are no less difficult."
Winston Churchill**

Define Your Problem

How do I define my problem? What caused you to think there was a problem? What is perplexing, baffling; confusing; complicated about this issue? What makes this issue a problem? How would I describe this problem or issue to my best friend? How critical is it to you that you find an answer to this problem? What about this problem takes away your peace? Is there a problem underneath this problem that is the real problem? What is that problem? What would be the opposite of having this problem?	

"The greatest challenge to any thinker is stating the problem in a way that will allow a solution."
Bertrand Russell

Define Your Problem

How do I define my problem?

What caused you to think there was a problem?

What is perplexing, baffling; confusing; complicated about this issue?

What makes this issue a problem?

How would I describe this problem or issue to my best friend?

How critical is it to you that you find an answer to this problem?

What about this problem takes away your peace?

Is there a problem underneath this problem that is the real problem? What is that problem?

What would be the opposite of having this problem?

"One of the tests of leadership is the ability to recognize a problem before it becomes an emergency."
Arnold Glasgow

Define Your Problem

How do I define my problem?

What caused you to think there was a problem?

What is perplexing, baffling; confusing; complicated about this issue?

What makes this issue a problem?

How would I describe this problem or issue to my best friend?

How critical is it to you that you find an answer to this problem?

What about this problem takes away your peace?

Is there a problem underneath this problem that is the real problem? What is that problem?

What would be the opposite of having this problem?

"When every physical and mental resource is focused, one's power to solve a problem multiplies tremendously."
Norman Vincent Peale

Define Your Problem

How do I define my problem?

What caused you to think there was a problem?

What is perplexing, baffling; confusing; complicated about this issue?

What makes this issue a problem?

How would I describe this problem or issue to my best friend?

How critical is it to you that you find an answer to this problem?

What about this problem takes away your peace?

Is there a problem underneath this problem that is the real problem? What is that problem?

What would be the opposite of having this problem?

"Again and again, the impossible problem is solved when we see that the problem is only a tough decision waiting to be made."
Robert Schuller

Define Your Problem

How do I define my problem?

What caused you to think there was a problem?

What is perplexing, baffling; confusing; complicated about this issue?

What makes this issue a problem?

How would I describe this problem or issue to my best friend?

How critical is it to you that you find an answer to this problem?

What about this problem takes away your peace?

Is there a problem underneath this problem that is the real problem? What is that problem?

What would be the opposite of having this problem?

"The first requisite of success is the ability to apply your physical and mental energies to one problem without growing weary."
Thomas Edison

Define Your Problem

How do I define my problem?

What caused you to think there was a problem?

What is perplexing, baffling; confusing; complicated about this issue?

What makes this issue a problem?

How would I describe this problem or issue to my best friend?

How critical is it to you that you find an answer to this problem?

What about this problem takes away your peace?

Is there a problem underneath this problem that is the real problem? What is that problem?

What would be the opposite of having this problem?

"Approach each new problem not with a view of finding what you hope will be there, but to get the truth, the realities that must be grappled with. You may not like what you find. In that case you are entitled to try to change it. But do not deceive yourself as to what you do find to be the facts of the situation."
Barnard Baruch

Define Your Problem

How do I define my problem?

What caused you to think there was a problem?

What is perplexing, baffling; confusing; complicated about this issue?

What makes this issue a problem?

How would I describe this problem or issue to my best friend?

How critical is it to you that you find an answer to this problem?

What about this problem takes away your peace?

Is there a problem underneath this problem that is the real problem? What is that problem?

What would be the opposite of having this problem?

"Have you got a problem? Do what you can where you are with what you've got."

Theodore Roosevelt

Define Your Problem

How do I define my problem?

What caused you to think there was a problem?

What is perplexing, baffling; confusing; complicated about this issue?

What makes this issue a problem?

How would I describe this problem or issue to my best friend?

How critical is it to you that you find an answer to this problem?

What about this problem takes away your peace?

Is there a problem underneath this problem that is the real problem? What is that problem?

What would be the opposite of having this problem?

How do I define my problem?

What caused you to think there was a problem?

What is perplexing, baffling; confusing; complicated about this issue?

What makes this issue a problem?

How would I describe this problem or issue to my best friend?

How critical is it to you that you find an answer to this problem?

What about this problem takes away your peace?

Is there a problem underneath this problem that is the real problem? What is that problem?

What would be the opposite of having this problem?

"He who asks a question may be a fool for five minutes, but he who never asks a question remains a fool forever."
Tom Connelly

Define Your Problem

How do I define my problem?

What caused you to think there was a problem?

What is perplexing, baffling; confusing; complicated about this issue?

What makes this issue a problem?

How would I describe this problem or issue to my best friend?

How critical is it to you that you find an answer to this problem?

What about this problem takes away your peace?

Is there a problem underneath this problem that is the real problem? What is that problem?

What would be the opposite of having this problem?

"Hot heads and cold hearts never solved anything"
Billy Graham

Define Your Problem

UNDERSTANDING MY EMOTIONS WORKSHEETS

Problem
Emotion
Analyze
Contemplate
Experiment

"It is better to know some of the questions than all of the answers."

James Thurber

Words for Emotions

Distress
Envy
Rivalry
Jealously
Compassion
Anxiety
Mourning
Sadness
Troubled
Grief
Lament
Depression
Frustration
Vexation
Despondency
Fear
Sluggishness
Shame
Fright
Timidity
Consternation
Bewilderment
Faintheartedness
Lust
Revenge
Rage
Hatred
Enmity
Wrath
Greed
Longing
Delight
Malice
Rapture
Smug
Ostentation
Joy
Surprise
Acceptance
Love
Care

Summarize the Problem Here:

____

____

____

____

____

E is for emotions. As you think about this problem, perplexity, or proposition what emotions are triggered inside of you? Use any words that help you get your emotions out. Draw pictures if it helps

____

____

____

____

____

____

____

____

____

____

Problem
Emotion
Analyze
Contemplate
Experiment

"It is better to know some of the questions
than all of the answers."
James Thurber

Words for Emotions

Distress
Envy
Rivalry
Jealously
Compassion
Anxiety
Mourning
Sadness
Troubled
Grief
Lament
Depression
Frustration
Vexation
Despondency
Fear
Sluggishness
Shame
Fright
Timidity
Consternation
Bewilderment
Faintheartedness
Lust
Revenge
Rage
Hatred
Enmity
Wrath
Greed
Longing
Delight
Malice
Rapture
Smug
Ostentation
Joy
Surprise
Acceptance
Love
Care

Summarize the Problem Here:

E is for emotions. As you think about this problem, perplexity, or proposition what emotions are triggered inside of you? Use any words that help you get your emotions out. Draw pictures if it helps

Problem
Emotion
Analyze
Contemplate
Experiment

"It is better to know some of the questions than all of the answers."

James Thurber

Words for Emotions

Distress
Envy
Rivalry
Jealously
Compassion
Anxiety
Mourning
Sadness
Troubled
Grief
Lament
Depression
Frustration
Vexation
Despondency
Fear
Sluggishness
Shame
Fright
Timidity
Consternation
Bewilderment
Faintheartedness
Lust
Revenge
Rage
Hatred
Enmity
Wrath
Greed
Longing
Delight
Malice
Rapture
Smug
Ostentation
Joy
Surprise
Acceptance
Love
Care

Summarize the Problem Here:

____

____

____

____

____

E is for emotions. As you think about this problem, perplexity, or proposition what emotions are triggered inside of you? Use any words that help you get your emotions out. Draw pictures if it helps

____

____

____

____

____

____

____

____

____

____

Problem
Emotion
Analyze
Contemplate
Experiment

"It is better to know some of the questions
than all of the answers."
James Thurber

Words for Emotions

Distress
Envy
Rivalry
Jealously
Compassion
Anxiety
Mourning
Sadness
Troubled
Grief
Lament
Depression
Frustration
Vexation
Despondency
Fear
Sluggishness
Shame
Fright
Timidity
Consternation
Bewilderment
Faintheartedness
Lust
Revenge
Rage
Hatred
Enmity
Wrath
Greed
Longing
Delight
Malice
Rapture
Smug
Ostentation
Joy
Surprise
Acceptance
Love
Care

Summarize the Problem Here:

____
____
____
____
____

E is for emotions. As you think about this problem, perplexity, or proposition what emotions are triggered inside of you? Use any words that help you get your emotions out. Draw pictures if it helps

____
____
____
____
____
____
____
____
____
____

Problem
Emotion
Analyze
Contemplate
Experiment

"It is better to know some of the questions than all of the answers."
James Thurber

Words for Emotions

Distress
Envy
Rivalry
Jealously
Compassion
Anxiety
Mourning
Sadness
Troubled
Grief
Lament
Depression
Frustration
Vexation
Despondency
Fear
Sluggishness
Shame
Fright
Timidity
Consternation
Bewilderment
Faintheartedness
Lust
Revenge
Rage
Hatred
Enmity
Wrath
Greed
Longing
Delight
Malice
Rapture
Smug
Ostentation
Joy
Surprise
Acceptance
Love
Care

Summarize the Problem Here:

____
____
____
____
____

E is for emotions. As you think about this problem, perplexity, or proposition what emotions are triggered inside of you? Use any words that help you get your emotions out. Draw pictures if it helps

____
____
____
____
____
____
____
____
____
____

Problem
Emotion
Analyze
Contemplate
Experiment

"It is better to know some of the questions
than all of the answers."
James Thurber

Words for Emotions

Distress
Envy
Rivalry
Jealously
Compassion
Anxiety
Mourning
Sadness
Troubled
Grief
Lament
Depression
Frustration
Vexation
Despondency
Fear
Sluggishness
Shame
Fright
Timidity
Consternation
Bewilderment
Faintheartedness
Lust
Revenge
Rage
Hatred
Enmity
Wrath
Greed
Longing
Delight
Malice
Rapture
Smug
Ostentation
Joy
Surprise
Acceptance
Love
Care

Summarize the Problem Here:

____

____

____

____

____

E is for emotions. As you think about this problem, perplexity, or proposition what emotions are triggered inside of you? Use any words that help you get your emotions out. Draw pictures if it helps

____

____

____

____

____

____

____

____

____

____

Problem
Emotion
Analyze
Contemplate
Experiment

"It is better to know some of the questions
than all of the answers."
James Thurber

Words for Emotions

Distress
Envy
Rivalry
Jealously
Compassion
Anxiety
Mourning
Sadness
Troubled
Grief
Lament
Depression
Frustration
Vexation
Despondency
Fear
Sluggishness
Shame
Fright
Timidity
Consternation
Bewilderment
Faintheartedness
Lust
Revenge
Rage
Hatred
Enmity
Wrath
Greed
Longing
Delight
Malice
Rapture
Smug
Ostentation
Joy
Surprise
Acceptance
Love
Care

Summarize the Problem Here:

____

____

____

____

____

E is for emotions. As you think about this problem, perplexity, or proposition what emotions are triggered inside of you? Use any words that help you get your emotions out. Draw pictures if it helps

____

____

____

____

____

____

____

____

____

____

Problem
Emotion
Analyze
Contemplate
Experiment

"It is better to know some of the questions
than all of the answers."
James Thurber

Words for Emotions

Distress
Envy
Rivalry
Jealously
Compassion
Anxiety
Mourning
Sadness
Troubled
Grief
Lament
Depression
Frustration
Vexation
Despondency
Fear
Sluggishness
Shame
Fright
Timidity
Consternation
Bewilderment
Faintheartedness
Lust
Revenge
Rage
Hatred
Enmity
Wrath
Greed
Longing
Delight
Malice
Rapture
Smug
Ostentation
Joy
Surprise
Acceptance
Love
Care

Summarize the Problem Here:

____

____

____

____

____

E is for emotions. As you think about this problem, perplexity, or proposition what emotions are triggered inside of you? Use any words that help you get your emotions out. Draw pictures if it helps

____

____

____

____

____

____

____

____

____

____

Problem
Emotion
Analyze
Contemplate
Experiment

"It is better to know some of the questions than all of the answers."
James Thurber

Words for Emotions

Distress
Envy
Rivalry
Jealously
Compassion
Anxiety
Mourning
Sadness
Troubled
Grief
Lament
Depression
Frustration
Vexation
Despondency
Fear
Sluggishness
Shame
Fright
Timidity
Consternation
Bewilderment
Faintheartedness
Lust
Revenge
Rage
Hatred
Enmity
Wrath
Greed
Longing
Delight
Malice
Rapture
Smug
Ostentation
Joy
Surprise
Acceptance
Love
Care

Summarize the Problem Here:

E is for emotions. As you think about this problem, perplexity, or proposition what emotions are triggered inside of you? Use any words that help you get your emotions out. Draw pictures if it helps

Problem
Emotion
Analyze
Contemplate
Experiment

"It is better to know some of the questions than all of the answers."
James Thurber

Words for Emotions

Distress
Envy
Rivalry
Jealously
Compassion
Anxiety
Mourning
Sadness
Troubled
Grief
Lament
Depression
Frustration
Vexation
Despondency
Fear
Sluggishness
Shame
Fright
Timidity
Consternation
Bewilderment
Faintheartedness
Lust
Revenge
Rage
Hatred
Enmity
Wrath
Greed
Longing
Delight
Malice
Rapture
Smug
Ostentation
Joy
Surprise
Acceptance
Love
Care

Summarize the Problem Here:

____

____

____

____

____

E is for emotions. As you think about this problem, perplexity, or proposition what emotions are triggered inside of you? Use any words that help you get your emotions out. Draw pictures if it helps

____

____

____

____

____

____

____

____

____

Problem
Emotion
Analyze
Contemplate
Experiment

"It is better to know some of the questions than all of the answers."
James Thurber

Words for Emotions

Distress
Envy
Rivalry
Jealously
Compassion
Anxiety
Mourning
Sadness
Troubled
Grief
Lament
Depression
Frustration
Vexation
Despondency
Fear
Sluggishness
Shame
Fright
Timidity
Consternation
Bewilderment
Faintheartedness
Lust
Revenge
Rage
Hatred
Enmity
Wrath
Greed
Longing
Delight
Malice
Rapture
Smug
Ostentation
Joy
Surprise
Acceptance
Love
Care

Summarize the Problem Here:

____

____

____

____

____

E is for emotions. As you think about this problem, perplexity, or proposition what emotions are triggered inside of you? Use any words that help you get your emotions out. Draw pictures if it helps

____

____

____

____

____

____

____

____

____

____

Problem
Emotion
Analyze
Contemplate
Experiment

"It is better to know some of the questions
than all of the answers."
James Thurber

Words for Emotions

Distress
Envy
Rivalry
Jealously
Compassion
Anxiety
Mourning
Sadness
Troubled
Grief
Lament
Depression
Frustration
Vexation
Despondency
Fear
Sluggishness
Shame
Fright
Timidity
Consternation
Bewilderment
Faintheartedness
Lust
Revenge
Rage
Hatred
Enmity
Wrath
Greed
Longing
Delight
Malice
Rapture
Smug
Ostentation
Joy
Surprise
Acceptance
Love
Care

Summarize the Problem Here:

____

____

____

____

____

E is for emotions. As you think about this problem, perplexity, or proposition what emotions are triggered inside of you? Use any words that help you get your emotions out. Draw pictures if it helps

____

____

____

____

____

____

____

____

____

____

Problem
Emotion
Analyze
Contemplate
Experiment

"It is better to know some of the questions than all of the answers."

James Thurber

Words for Emotions

Distress
Envy
Rivalry
Jealously
Compassion
Anxiety
Mourning
Sadness
Troubled
Grief
Lament
Depression
Frustration
Vexation
Despondency
Fear
Sluggishness
Shame
Fright
Timidity
Consternation
Bewilderment
Faintheartedness
Lust
Revenge
Rage
Hatred
Enmity
Wrath
Greed
Longing
Delight
Malice
Rapture
Smug
Ostentation
Joy
Surprise
Acceptance
Love
Care

Summarize the Problem Here:

____

____

____

____

____

E is for emotions. As you think about this problem, perplexity, or proposition what emotions are triggered inside of you? Use any words that help you get your emotions out. Draw pictures if it helps

____

____

____

____

____

____

____

____

____

____

Problem
Emotion
Analyze
Contemplate
Experiment

"It is better to know some of the questions
than all of the answers."
James Thurber

Words for Emotions

Distress
Envy
Rivalry
Jealously
Compassion
Anxiety
Mourning
Sadness
Troubled
Grief
Lament
Depression
Frustration
Vexation
Despondency
Fear
Sluggishness
Shame
Fright
Timidity
Consternation
Bewilderment
Faintheartedness
Lust
Revenge
Rage
Hatred
Enmity
Wrath
Greed
Longing
Delight
Malice
Rapture
Smug
Ostentation
Joy
Surprise
Acceptance
Love
Care

Summarize the Problem Here:

____

____

____

____

____

E is for emotions. As you think about this problem, perplexity, or proposition what emotions are triggered inside of you? Use any words that help you get your emotions out. Draw pictures if it helps

____

____

____

____

____

____

____

____

____

____

Problem
Emotion
Analyze
Contemplate
Experiment

"It is better to know some of the questions than all of the answers."
James Thurber

Words for Emotions

Distress
Envy
Rivalry
Jealously
Compassion
Anxiety
Mourning
Sadness
Troubled
Grief
Lament
Depression
Frustration
Vexation
Despondency
Fear
Sluggishness
Shame
Fright
Timidity
Consternation
Bewilderment
Faintheartedness
Lust
Revenge
Rage
Hatred
Enmity
Wrath
Greed
Longing
Delight
Malice
Rapture
Smug
Ostentation
Joy
Surprise
Acceptance
Love
Care

Summarize the Problem Here:

____

____

____

____

____

E is for emotions. As you think about this problem, perplexity, or proposition what emotions are triggered inside of you? Use any words that help you get your emotions out. Draw pictures if it helps

____

____

____

____

____

____

____

____

____

____

Problem
Emotion
Analyze
Contemplate
Experiment

"It is better to know some of the questions
than all of the answers."
James Thurber

Words for Emotions

Distress
Envy
Rivalry
Jealously
Compassion
Anxiety
Mourning
Sadness
Troubled
Grief
Lament
Depression
Frustration
Vexation
Despondency
Fear
Sluggishness
Shame
Fright
Timidity
Consternation
Bewilderment
Faintheartedness
Lust
Revenge
Rage
Hatred
Enmity
Wrath
Greed
Longing
Delight
Malice
Rapture
Smug
Ostentation
Joy
Surprise
Acceptance
Love
Care

Summarize the Problem Here:

____

____

____

____

____

E is for emotions. As you think about this problem, perplexity, or proposition what emotions are triggered inside of you? Use any words that help you get your emotions out. Draw pictures if it helps

____

____

____

____

____

____

____

____

____

____

Analyze the Problem

Problem
Emotion
Analyze
Contemplate
Experiment

Summarize the Problem Here:

____

____

____

____

Summarize the Key Emotions Here:

____

____

____

____

Analyze the Problem by answering the following

Analyze - To subject to analysis; to resolve (anything complex) into its elements; to separate into the constituent parts, for the purpose of an examination of each separately; to examine in such a manner as to ascertain the elements or nature of the thing examined; as, to analyze a fossil substance; to analyze a sentence or a word; to analyze an action to ascertain its morality.

Analysis
Analysis means literally to break a complex problem down into smaller, more manageable "independent" parts for the purposes of examination — with the hope that solving these smaller parts will lead to a solution of the more complex problem as well.

Thoughts:

PROBLEM ANALYSIS QUESTIONS SHEETS

Analysis Questions:

How is my past impacting the present problem?

What are all the "parts" of this problem?

What is the “chemistry” or “life dynamic” of this problem? How does this problem keep reoccurring? Is there a “system” which gives life to the problem?

What are all the possible answers to the problem or idea that is being considered?

List the best answers. Do not consider more than six possible answers and the strengths and weakness of each.

Possible Areas	Strengths	Weaknesses

Analysis Questions:

How is my past impacting the present problem?

____

____

____

____

____

What are all the "parts" of this problem?

____

____

____

____

____

____

____

____

____

____

____

____

____

____

____

____

____

What is the "chemistry" or "life dynamic" of this problem? How does this problem keep reoccurring? Is there a "system" which gives life to the problem?

What are all the possible answers to the problem or idea that is being considered?

List the best answers. Do not consider more than six possible answers and the strengths and weakness of each.

Possible Areas	Strengths	Weaknesses

Analysis Questions:

How is my past impacting the present problem?

____

____

____

____

____

What are all the "parts" of this problem?

____

____

____

____

____

____

____

____

____

____

____

____

____

____

____

____

____

What is the "chemistry" or "life dynamic" of this problem? How does this problem keep reoccurring? Is there a "system" which gives life to the problem?

What are all the possible answers to the problem or idea that is being considered?

List the best answers. Do not consider more than six possible answers and the strengths and weakness of each.

Possible Areas	Strengths	Weaknesses

Analysis Questions:

How is my past impacting the present problem?

What are all the “parts” of this problem?

What is the “chemistry” or “life dynamic” of this problem? How does this problem keep reoccurring? Is there a “system” which gives life to the problem?

What are all the possible answers to the problem or idea that is being considered?

List the best answers. Do not consider more than six possible answers and the strengths and weakness of each.

Possible Areas	Strengths	Weaknesses

Analysis Questions:

How is my past impacting the present problem?

What are all the “parts” of this problem?

What is the “chemistry” or “life dynamic” of this problem? How does this problem keep reoccurring? Is there a “system” which gives life to the problem?

What are all the possible answers to the problem or idea that is being considered?

List the best answers. Do not consider more than six possible answers and the strengths and weakness of each.

Possible Areas	**Strengths**	**Weaknesses**

Analysis Questions:

How is my past impacting the present problem?

What are all the “parts” of this problem?

What is the "chemistry" or "life dynamic" of this problem? How does this problem keep reoccurring? Is there a "system" which gives life to the problem?

What are all the possible answers to the problem or idea that is being considered?

List the best answers. Do not consider more than six possible answers and the strengths and weakness of each.

Possible Areas	Strengths	Weaknesses

Analysis Questions:

How is my past impacting the present problem?

____

____

____

____

____

What are all the "parts" of this problem?

____

____

____

____

____

____

____

____

____

____

____

____

____

____

____

____

____

What is the "chemistry" or "life dynamic" of this problem? How does this problem keep reoccurring? Is there a "system" which gives life to the problem?

What are all the possible answers to the problem or idea that is being considered?

List the best answers. Do not consider more than six possible answers and the strengths and weakness of each.

Possible Areas	**Strengths**	**Weaknesses**

Analysis Questions:

How is my past impacting the present problem?

What are all the "parts" of this problem?

What is the "chemistry" or "life dynamic" of this problem? How does this problem keep reoccurring? Is there a "system" which gives life to the problem?

What are all the possible answers to the problem or idea that is being considered?

List the best answers. Do not consider more than six possible answers and the strengths and weakness of each.

Possible Areas	Strengths	Weaknesses

Analysis Questions:

How is my past impacting the present problem?

What are all the "parts" of this problem?

What is the "chemistry" or "life dynamic" of this problem? How does this problem keep reoccurring? Is there a "system" which gives life to the problem?

What are all the possible answers to the problem or idea that is being considered?

List the best answers. Do not consider more than six possible answers and the strengths and weakness of each.

Possible Areas	Strengths	Weaknesses

Analysis Questions:

How is my past impacting the present problem?

____

____

____

____

____

What are all the "parts" of this problem?

____

____

____

____

____

____

____

____

____

____

____

____

____

____

____

____

____

What is the "chemistry" or "life dynamic" of this problem? How does this problem keep reoccurring? Is there a "system" which gives life to the problem?

What are all the possible answers to the problem or idea that is being considered?

List the best answers. Do not consider more than six possible answers and the strengths and weakness of each.

Possible Areas	**Strengths**	**Weaknesses**

Analysis Questions:

How is my past impacting the present problem?

____

____

____

____

____

What are all the "parts" of this problem?

____

____

____

____

____

____

____

____

____

____

____

____

____

____

____

____

____

What is the "chemistry" or "life dynamic" of this problem? How does this problem keep reoccurring? Is there a "system" which gives life to the problem?

What are all the possible answers to the problem or idea that is being considered?

List the best answers. Do not consider more than six possible answers and the strengths and weakness of each.

Possible Areas	Strengths	Weaknesses

CONTEMPLATION QUESTIONS

Contemplate the Answer

Problem **Emotion** **Analyze** **Contemplate** **Experiment**

Summarize the Problem Here:

____

____

____

Summarize the Key Emotions Here:

____

____

List your analysis of the best possible answers here:

____

____

____

____

What does it mean to contemplate?

To look at on all sides or in all its bearings; to view or consider with continued attention; to regard with deliberate care; to meditate on and seek to find peace in an answer.

Contemplation Questions:

Which of the possible answers do you feel is the best in reality?

____

____

____

____

____

____

Why?

____

____

____

On a scale between 1-100, how confident are you of this answer?
(1 is no confidence and 100 is complete confidence)

1	10	20	30	40	50	60	70	80	90	100

What impact will actually applying the answer have on your life?

Is this answer a "win/win"solution that honors everyone involved?

Is this solution a sane, stable, spiritual solution? Defend your answer:

Is this what Jesus would do in your circumstances? Why or why not?

Free Contemplation

Contemplate the Answer

Problem **Emotion** **Analyze** **Contemplate** **Experiment**

Summarize the Problem Here:

Summarize the Key Emotions Here:

List your analysis of the best possible answers here:

What does it mean to contemplate?

To look at on all sides or in all its bearings; to view or consider with continued attention; to regard with deliberate care; to meditate on and seek to find peace in an answer.

Contemplation Questions:

Which of the possible answers do you feel is the best in reality?

Why?

On a scale between 1-100, how confident are you of this answer?
(1 is no confidence and 100 is complete confidence)

1	10	20	30	40	50	60	70	80	90	100

What impact will actually applying the answer have on your life?

____

____

____

____

Is this answer a "win/win"solution that honors everyone involved?

____

____

____

____

Is this solution a sane, stable, spiritual solution? Defend your answer:

____

____

____

____

____

____

____

____

Is this what Jesus would do in your circumstances? Why or why not?

Free Contemplation

Contemplate the Answer

Problem **Emotion** **Analyze** **Contemplate** **Experiment**

Summarize the Problem Here:

____

____

____

Summarize the Key Emotions Here:

____

____

List your analysis of the best possible answers here:

____

____

____

____

What does it mean to contemplate?

> *To look at on all sides or in all its bearings; to view or consider with continued attention; to regard with deliberate care; to meditate on and seek to find peace in an answer.*

Contemplation Questions:

Which of the possible answers do you feel is the best in reality?

____

____

____

____

____

____

Why?

____

____

____

On a scale between 1-100, how confident are you of this answer? (1 is no confidence and 100 is complete confidence)

1	10	20	30	40	50	60	70	80	90	100

What impact will actually applying the answer have on your life?

Is this answer a "win/win"solution that honors everyone involved?

Is this solution a sane, stable, spiritual solution? Defend your answer:

Is this what Jesus would do in your circumstances? Why or why not?

Free Contemplation

Contemplate the Answer

Problem **Emotion** **Analyze** **Contemplate** **Experiment**

Summarize the Problem Here:

Summarize the Key Emotions Here:

List your analysis of the best possible answers here:

What does it mean to contemplate?

To look at on all sides or in all its bearings; to view or consider with continued attention; to regard with deliberate care; to meditate on and seek to find peace in an answer.

Contemplation Questions:

Which of the possible answers do you feel is the best in reality?

Why?

On a scale between 1-100, how confident are you of this answer? (1 is no confidence and 100 is complete confidence)

1	10	20	30	40	50	60	70	80	90	100

What impact will actually applying the answer have on your life?

Is this answer a "win/win"solution that honors everyone involved?

Is this solution a sane, stable, spiritual solution? Defend your answer:

Is this what Jesus would do in your circumstances? Why or why not?

Free Contemplation

Contemplate the Answer

Problem
Emotion
Analyze
Contemplate
Experiment

Summarize the Problem Here:

____

____

____

Summarize the Key Emotions Here:

____

____

List your analysis of the best possible answers here:

____

____

____

____

What does it mean to contemplate?

To look at on all sides or in all its bearings; to view or consider with continued attention; to regard with deliberate care; to meditate on and seek to find peace in an answer.

Contemplation Questions:

Which of the possible answers do you feel is the best in reality?

____

____

____

____

____

____

Why?

____

____

____

On a scale between 1-100, how confident are you of this answer? (1 is no confidence and 100 is complete confidence)

1	10	20	30	40	50	60	70	80	90	100

What impact will actually applying the answer have on your life?

Is this answer a "win/win"solution that honors everyone involved?

Is this solution a sane, stable, spiritual solution? Defend your answer:

Is this what Jesus would do in your circumstances? Why or why not?

Free Contemplation

Contemplate the Answer

Problem **Emotion** **Analyze** **Contemplate** **Experiment**

Summarize the Problem Here:

____

____

____

Summarize the Key Emotions Here:

____

____

List your analysis of the best possible answers here:

____

____

____

____

What does it mean to contemplate?

> *To look at on all sides or in all its bearings; to view or consider with continued attention; to regard with deliberate care; to meditate on and seek to find peace in an answer.*

Contemplation Questions:

Which of the possible answers do you feel is the best in reality?

____

____

____

____

____

____

Why?

____

____

____

On a scale between 1-100, how confident are you of this answer? (1 is no confidence and 100 is complete confidence)

1	10	20	30	40	50	60	70	80	90	100

What impact will actually applying the answer have on your life?

____

____

____

____

Is this answer a "win/win"solution that honors everyone involved?

____

____

____

____

Is this solution a sane, stable, spiritual solution? Defend your answer:

____

____

____

____

____

____

____

____

Is this what Jesus would do in your circumstances? Why or why not?

Free Contemplation

Contemplate the Answer

Problem **Emotion** **Analyze** **Contemplate** **Experiment**

Summarize the Problem Here:

____

____

____

Summarize the Key Emotions Here:

____

____

List your analysis of the best possible answers here:

____

____

____

____

What does it mean to contemplate?

To look at on all sides or in all its bearings; to view or consider with continued attention; to regard with deliberate care; to meditate on and seek to find peace in an answer.

Contemplation Questions:

Which of the possible answers do you feel is the best in reality?

____

____

____

____

____

____

Why?

____

____

____

On a scale between 1-100, how confident are you of this answer? (1 is no confidence and 100 is complete confidence)

1	10	20	30	40	50	60	70	80	90	100

What impact will actually applying the answer have on your life?

Is this answer a "win/win"solution that honors everyone involved?

Is this solution a sane, stable, spiritual solution? Defend your answer:

Is this what Jesus would do in your circumstances? Why or why not?

Free Contemplation

Contemplate the Answer

Problem Emotion Analyze Contemplate Experiment

Summarize the Problem Here:

Summarize the Key Emotions Here:

List your analysis of the best possible answers here:

What does it mean to contemplate?

To look at on all sides or in all its bearings; to view or consider with continued attention; to regard with deliberate care; to meditate on and seek to find peace in an answer.

Contemplation Questions:

Which of the possible answers do you feel is the best in reality?

Why?

On a scale between 1-100, how confident are you of this answer? (1 is no confidence and 100 is complete confidence)

1	10	20	30	40	50	60	70	80	90	100

What impact will actually applying the answer have on your life?

____

____

____

____

Is this answer a “win/win”solution that honors everyone involved?

____

____

____

____

Is this solution a sane, stable, spiritual solution? Defend your answer:

____

____

____

____

____

____

____

____

Is this what Jesus would do in your circumstances? Why or why not?

Free Contemplation

Contemplate the Answer

Problem **Emotion** **Analyze** **Contemplate** **Experiment**

Summarize the Problem Here:

____

____

____

Summarize the Key Emotions Here:

____

____

List your analysis of the best possible answers here:

____

____

____

____

What does it mean to contemplate?

> *To look at on all sides or in all its bearings; to view or consider with continued attention; to regard with deliberate care; to meditate on and seek to find peace in an answer.*

Contemplation Questions:

Which of the possible answers do you feel is the best in reality?

____

____

____

____

____

____

Why?

____

____

____

On a scale between 1-100, how confident are you of this answer?
(1 is no confidence and 100 is complete confidence)

1	10	20	30	40	50	60	70	80	90	100

What impact will actually applying the answer have on your life?

Is this answer a "win/win"solution that honors everyone involved?

Is this solution a sane, stable, spiritual solution? Defend your answer:

Is this what Jesus would do in your circumstances? Why or why not?

Free Contemplation

Contemplate the Answer

Problem
Emotion
Analyze
Contemplate
Experiment

Summarize the Problem Here:

Summarize the Key Emotions Here:

List your analysis of the best possible answers here:

What does it mean to contemplate?

To look at on all sides or in all its bearings; to view or consider with continued attention; to regard with deliberate care; to meditate on and seek to find peace in an answer.

Contemplation Questions:

Which of the possible answers do you feel is the best in reality?

Why?

On a scale between 1-100, how confident are you of this answer? (1 is no confidence and 100 is complete confidence)

1	10	20	30	40	50	60	70	80	90	100

What impact will actually applying the answer have on your life?

____

____

____

____

Is this answer a "win/win"solution that honors everyone involved?

____

____

____

____

Is this solution a sane, stable, spiritual solution? Defend your answer:

____

____

____

____

____

____

____

____

Is this what Jesus would do in your circumstances? Why or why not?

Free Contemplation

Contemplate the Answer

Problem **Emotion** **Analyze** **Contemplate** **Experiment**

Summarize the Problem Here:

____

____

____

Summarize the Key Emotions Here:

____

____

List your analysis of the best possible answers here:

____

____

____

____

What does it mean to contemplate?

To look at on all sides or in all its bearings; to view or consider with continued attention; to regard with deliberate care; to meditate on and seek to find peace in an answer.

Contemplation Questions:

Which of the possible answers do you feel is the best in reality?

____

____

____

____

____

____

Why?

____

____

____

On a scale between 1-100, how confident are you of this answer?
(1 is no confidence and 100 is complete confidence)

1	10	20	30	40	50	60	70	80	90	100

What impact will actually applying the answer have on your life?

Is this answer a "win/win"solution that honors everyone involved?

Is this solution a sane, stable, spiritual solution? Defend your answer:

Is this what Jesus would do in your circumstances? Why or why not?

Free Contemplation

Contemplate the Answer

Problem
Emotion
Analyze
Contemplate
Experiment

Summarize the Problem Here:

____

____

____

Summarize the Key Emotions Here:

____

____

List your analysis of the best possible answers here:

____

____

____

____

What does it mean to contemplate?

To look at on all sides or in all its bearings; to view or consider with continued attention; to regard with deliberate care; to meditate on and seek to find peace in an answer.

Contemplation Questions:

Which of the possible answers do you feel is the best in reality?

____

____

____

____

____

____

Why?

____

____

____

On a scale between 1-100, how confident are you of this answer?
(1 is no confidence and 100 is complete confidence)

1	10	20	30	40	50	60	70	80	90	100

What impact will actually applying the answer have on your life?

____

____

____

____

Is this answer a "win/win"solution that honors everyone involved?

____

____

____

____

Is this solution a sane, stable, spiritual solution? Defend your answer:

____

____

____

____

____

____

____

____

Is this what Jesus would do in your circumstances? Why or why not?

Free Contemplation

Experiment

In the scientific method, an experiment [Latin: ex- periri, "of (or from) trying"] is a set of observations performed in the context of solving a particular problem or question, to support or falsify a hypothesis, theory, idea, or research concerning the issue under analysis.

Elements of a "S.M.A.R.T." Experiment
Specific
Measurable
Attainable
Realistic
Time Defined

Specific: Who, what, where, which, when, why

Measurable: Concrete ways of measuring progress and success

Attainable: You have a real commitment to doing the experiment and reaching the positive goal of the experiment

Realistic: Your experiment can be done by you in your world. It is not an illusion of your mind but a real concrete possibility.

Time Defined: The experiment should have a definite start date and a date for when you will evaluate its effectiveness. Remember that you must give enough time to really see significant changes.

Notes:

How could I practically test my solution? How do I take this thinking and put it into practice?

How could I practically test my solution? How do I take this thinking and put it into practice?

How could I practically test my solution? How do I take this thinking and put it into practice?

How could I practically test my solution? How do I take this thinking and put it into practice?

How could I practically test my solution? How do I take this thinking and put it into practice?

How could I practically test my solution? How do I take this thinking and put it into practice?

How could I practically test my solution? How do I take this thinking and put it into practice?

How could I practically test my solution? How do I take this thinking and put it into practice?

How could I practically test my solution? How do I take this thinking and put it into practice?

How could I practically test my solution? How do I take this thinking and put it into practice?

How could I practically test my solution? How do I take this thinking and put it into practice?

How could I practically test my solution? How do I take this thinking and put it into practice?

How could I practically test my solution? How do I take this thinking and put it into practice?

How could I practically test my solution? How do I take this thinking and put it into practice?

FREE CONTEMPLATION

FREE CONTEMPLATION

FREE CONTEMPLATION

FREE CONTEMPLATION

FREE CONTEMPLATION

FREE CONTEMPLATION

FREE CONTEMPLATION

FREE CONTEMPLATION

FREE CONTEMPLATION

FREE CONTEMPLATION

FREE CONTEMPLATION

Books on How To Journal [1]

Journaling as a Spiritual Practice: *Encountering God Through Attentive,* by Helen Cepero

Spiritual Journaling: Recording Your Journey Toward God (*Spiritual Formation Study Guides*), by Richard Peace

The Many Faces of Journaling: *Topics &: Techniques for Personal Journal,* by Linda C. Senn

Complete Idiot's Guide to Journaling, by Joan Neubauer

Journal to the Self: *Twenty-Two Paths to Personal Growth: Open the Door to Self-Understanding by Writing, Reading, and Creating a Journal of Your Life*, by Kathleen Adam

Plato, Not Prozac! *Applying Eternal Wisdom to Everyday Problems*, by Lou Marinoff (Paperback - Aug 1, 2000) - Not a book on journaling but on how to think clearly and one of the inspirations for this journal.

---

[1] I do not support every idea or practice in these books. However, they can be helpful in developing a life of journaling.

24832018R00085

Made in the USA
Lexington, KY
02 August 2013